Looking Good

Written by Christine Green
Illustrated by Mandy Doyle

© 1993 Henderson Publishing Limited

Henderson
Woodbridge, England *Publishing*

LOOK GOOD, FEEL GREAT

There is no other piece of machinery to match the human body. But how well it operates largely depends on how well it is maintained and fuelled. A combination of sensible eating, fresh air, regular exercise and adequate rest will ensure your body functions, and looks, its best.

Healthy Eating

What we fuel our bodies with is very important. This is one reason why our daily diet should contain a balance of protein, carbohydrates, fat, vitamins, and minerals, particularly whilst growing.

Protein - Important for growth. Present in bananas, meat, liver, poultry, fish, cheese, milk, nuts, eggs, etc.

Carbohydrates - Energy giving. Present in fruit, salads, sugar, vegetables and flour, etc.

Fat - Helps good general health. Makes for shiny hair and clear skin. Because fats are also full of calories, everyone must take care not to eat too much fatty food. Choose products containing unsaturated fats. These fats are broken down easily by your body, so won't clog your blood. Fats are present in cooking oil, butter, red meat, milk, cheese and other dairy products, whereas olive oil and sunflower margarine contain the polyunsaturates, which are so much better for you.

Vitamins - Needed for good health and are available in fresh foods. Unfortunately, many vitamins are destroyed during the cooking process.

Minerals - Needed to maintain good health. These are present in most everyday foods but, like vitamins, they can be destroyed during the cooking process.

Roughage - Important in any healthy diet. Those foods which contain fibre aid the work of the intestine in helping the body to dispose of waste. This is present in fresh fruit, whole-grain pasta and bread, etc

Everyone enjoys eating a hamburger and chips or a bar of chocolate now and again and why not? They're tasty and they're okay - just so long as you don't eat them in place of a nourishing meal on a regular basis.

Excellent foods to eat:- Apples, oranges, grapes, lettuce, cauliflower, Brussel sprouts, tomatoes, cottage cheese, chicken, turkey, cod.

Good foods to eat:-
Cheese, bacon, ham, eggs, tuna, grilled sausages, milk, cream, peanut butter, bananas, baked beans, margarine, potatoes (jacket, baked or boiled), wholemeal cereals, peas.

Foods to eat just a little of:- Fried foods including fish, sausage rolls, processed meat, white bread/buns, biscuits, cakes, sweets, fizzy drink, pies, jam, crisps, chips.

Tips
* Never skip breakfast, always leave for school with something in your stomach, even if it is just a piece of fruit.
* Ask mum to change to using semi-skimmed milk for a healthier all-round family diet.
* Try to eat a varied diet to include items from each food group every day.
* Don't diet. Eat sensibly. If you do have a weight problem, it's best to talk to your doctor about it first.
* Most people enjoy sweets or chocolate sometimes. Don't get into the habit of eating them too often. Try to make a little go a long way!
* Make sure you eat at least one piece of fresh fruit each day.

BODY TALK

It's not very pleasant standing next to someone who doesn't smell fresh, so personal hygiene is very important and should include a daily wash of your body and clean clothes to keep away any stale, unpleasant odours.

Sweat Glands

Our body is covered with thousands of sweat glands (eccrine). These are found on the soles of your feet, palms of hands, the face and also under the arms. Their job is to emit water from our body into the atmosphere.

After exercising, perhaps doing some energetic sport, the body automatically sweats more. This sweating process is a normal healthy function of your body and part of the cooling system which helps keep the body at the correct temperature.

As you get older, usually in your early teens, larger glands under the arms and around the genital areas, called apocrine, are brought into action. They react when you feel emotionally upset or are in a worrying situation (like before an exam).

Sweat

When fresh, sweat has no smell, but after several hours' contact with the bacteria that is always present on the skin, the result can be a rather unpleasant body odour.

Daily Washing

The best way to avoid this unfriendly smell is a daily bath or shower. A good all-over wash will work, too, if you pay particular attention to underarms, the feet, and more intimate parts of the body.

Deodorants

It probably won't be necessary to use a deodorant until you're at least eleven or even older. Once those apocrine glands move into action, it's best to be safe! There are two types of deodorant:
Anti-perspirants - prevent some of the sweat from reaching the surface of the skin, helping to prevent wetness and smell.
Deodorants - stop the stale smell by fighting the bacteria, but don't stop the wetness that occurs.

Both deodorants and anti-perspirants are available in spray, roll-on, creams and sticks. There are lots on sale to suit different skin types. For example, some are perfumed whilst others are not. Some people may have an allergic reaction to a brand of deodorant or anti-perspirant. If it causes a skin rash, try a milder, unperfumed one instead.

If you find sweating is a problem even with an antiperspirant, ask your doctor for some advice .

Sleep

Sleep is important for giving your body time to rest and repair itself after a hard day's work - or play! Energy output, age and your body's requirements play a large part in determining how much sleep you need. For example, an elderly person needs less sleep than a baby or young child. On average between six and ten hours a night is necessary for most people and many have a regular pattern of eight hours.

Exercise

A healthy body helps to keep your mind in good shape. It's perfectly true! Exercise improves and tones up your muscles. It increases your energy, helps you to relax and speeds up the circulation of aired blood which supplies nourishment to all parts of the body. That's what gives people a general healthy feeling!

Types of Exercise

Exercise should be enjoyable - something which all the family can join in with.

* The cheapest and one of the most relaxing forms of exercise is a good brisk walk.

* Gymnastics are great fun, or you may prefer jogging, cycling or even dancing!

* Swimming is a firm favourite and a good all round exercise. It's especially good for keeping limbs and muscles supple. Many swimming baths have special family sessions.

* Exercising with company is really good fun. If you don't take part in a group exercise at least once a week, check out some clubs in your area or at school. They're too good to miss.

Teeth

We are all born with potentially healthy teeth, but keeping them healthy is not always so easy. Be aware of what you eat, and learn how to clean your teeth properly.

A regular trip to your dentist will add the finishing touches to your Dental Fitness Programme!

Plaque

The biggest enemy of teeth is plaque, a sticky substance which gathers on the teeth when sugar is present in the mouth. Another enemy is bacteria. This flourishes on the plaque and eats away into the teeth and gums. In time it causes tooth decay and that is why people loose their teeth.

To cut down on these sorts of dental problems, reduce your sugar intake. That doesn't necessarily mean cutting out sweets altogether; simply brush your teeth after eating them. And if you're feeling peckish, grab an apple or a crunchy vegetable instead of chocolate or sweets.

Cleaning Teeth

Clean teeth both morning and night, paying particular attention to the back of the teeth.

Dental Floss - Often particles of food become lodged in between the teeth, so use dental floss to shift them.

Plaque Disclosing tablet - As it dissolves and mixes with the mouth saliva, the dye will identify the remaining plaque where more brushing is required. But don't brush too hard or you'll damage your gums. Healthy gums are vital to healthy teeth.

Fluoride - is important to combat decay, so buy a toothpaste with added fluoride for extra protection.

Tooth Trouble?

Coloured teeth - Don't worry if your teeth aren't lily white; often the healthiest are yellowish in colour.

Loose tooth - Accidents happen, and often during sports events. If you find yourself with a dislodged tooth, don't panic. If it is still in the socket, try to keep it there and go to your dentist who may be able to replant it!

Brace - Teeth out of line can be saved by wearing a brace for a length of time. Nowadays braces are available in many new fashion colours, but their job is a very important one.

Remember, your dentist is your friend, so keep your appointments and follow his or her advice. Look after your teeth and you shouldn't have many problems.

SKIN

Did you know skin is the hardest working organ of the human body? It is also the largest and, next to the brain, it's by far the most complex. Your skin has several important functions:- to prevent your body from dehydrating, to allow you to feel various temperatures, to maintain body temperature, and to protect your muscles from damage and infection.

Your skin is made up of many thin layers. The most important are these:

Epidermis - is the layer of skin you can see. It is made up of many sub-layers. It is in one of these that new skin cells are created.

Dermis - lies under the epidermis. This is the storehouse of all the essential things required to keep our skin healthy; sweat glands to maintain a constant body temperature, sebaceous glands to oil the skin and stop it from drying out, blood vessels to transport blood and oxygen to the skin, hair follicles, and nerve endings which relay messages about touch and pain to the brain.

Epidermis

Dermis

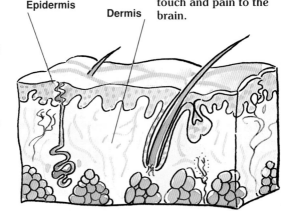

Skin Types

A simple skin care routine is really worth the effort, but you need to know your own skin type.

Dry - Does you skin feel tight after washing? If it is dry, it may flake or chap and feel sensitive.

Sensitive - Skin reacts to many external influences, like the sun and cold wind. It can be allergic to make-up, scents or soaps. There are many non-irritant (hypo-allergenic) products available from your chemist to cleanse and care for sensitive skin.

Oily - You will notice that your skin appears shiny and is prone to blackheads.

Normal - Maybe your skin is clear and smooth, in which case you probably have normal skin. Even good skin needs care to preserve its look for many years to come.

Combination - Many people have this type of skin. It usually means a slightly oily patch around the nose and centre of the forehead, with other parts of the face being drier. This type needs careful attention to restore a more normal balance.

Taking Care of Your Skin

Now you know your skin type, learn how to take care of it and ensure you always have a clear, healthy, complexion.

Cleansing

Everyday dirt and grime from the air clings to your skin, so cleaning it is important. For many this simply means washing with soap and water. However, ordinary soap and water may leave your skin feeling tight and dry. If so, there are alternatives, such as water active creams and facial cleansing bars. There are also many hypo-allergenic soaps for sensitive and problem skins.

How To Cleanse Your Face

* Keep the cleanser away from the eye area. Apply lotion on to a piece of cotton or tissue and apply it over the face working out towards the hairline and under the jawline.
* Using a fresh piece of cotton wool for each area of the face to remove the cleanser, again working out towards the hairline.

Tip

* You don't have to spend money on good skin care - remember, there's always a good, natural alternative. Raw potato rubbed over the face makes a good facial cleanser!

Deep Cleansing

This method is designed to reach parts of the skin that ordinary daily cleansing fails to do. Generally, it is best not to overdo it and so most products will recommend that you use them once a week.

Face Mask - A special treat for the skin! They come in gels and creams, designed to cleanse, tone, nourish or moisturise, leaving it feeling wonderful. Some (usually clay-based) set hard and need careful removing with warm water, while others stay fluid and may only take three minutes. Choose one suitable for your skin and follow the instructions. A mask is particularly good to use just before a special occasion, like a party,

Tip
* You can find the ingredients of a natural face mask in your own kitchen!

Egg - whip up the egg white and, avoiding the eye area, apply it over the face. Leave for 10 minutes then wash off with tepid water.

Yoghurt - plain is great. Simply lather it in, let it dry and rinse off. Plain yoghurt is ideal as a milky cleanser, too. Work into skin and rinse.

Facial Sauna - Fill a bowl with boiling water. Drape a towel over your head and hold it about 8 inches (20cm) over the bowl. Stay there for approximately 10-20 minutes. (Don't go out into cold air for at least half an hour after this treatment.)

Toning

A toner is used after cleansing the face with cream to make sure every bit of the cleanser has been removed. It also helps to close up the pores, improve the feeling of your skin and increase the skin's circulation. Don't buy a toner which contains astringents unless you have very oily skin. Harsh astringents will dry up the natural oils which healthy skin needs to stay soft and smooth.

How To Tone Your Face

1) Soak a piece of cotton wool in some water and squeeze out surplus.

2) Pour some toner on to the cotton wool and, avoiding the eye area, wipe it over your face working out toward the hairline.

Tips

* By wetting the cotton wool before adding the toner you will ensure that not too much toner is absorbed on to the cotton wool.
* Vinegar diluted one part to 8 parts of water is a super skin tonic.

Moisturising

After cleansing and toning your face, the next step is to moisturise it. Moisturisers are available in lotion or cream, and prevent the skin from losing its natural moisture.

How To Moisturise Your Skin

1) Dot the cream around your face.

2) Gently massage it in, making sure it is all absorbed.

There are many different types of cleansers, toners and moisturisers available, and it is important to buy one to suit your skin type. People with sensitive skin should look out for one of the hypo-allergenic cosmetics from which perfume and other irritants have been excluded. There are many chemists and department stores which will offer you free advice on your skin type, so don't be afraid to ask.

Spots
Your body will undergo many changes during adolescence. Because of this, spots will be a common problem for teenagers, boys and girls alike.

Teenage Acne
Teenage acne is caused by an imbalance in the hormones - which doesn't help much, if you have it, does it? It's another difficult part of growing up. However, often acne can be cleared up effectively by washing the face using a very mild soap.

A severe case of acne ought to be treated by a Doctor who will prescribe a specially medicated preparation to use, so don't just put up with it!

Tips
* Never pick or squeeze spots, as this can lead to infection when spots may spread.

* Conceal an odd spot with antiseptic tinted sticks. These dry out the spot and still allow you to apply make up - or look good without it, if you prefer.

* If you have just a single spot, soak a cotton bud in lemon juice and carefully wipe that area of your face.

* Always remove make-up before going to bed.

MAKE-UP

No make-up will improve the natural beauty of young skin. But when you become a teenager, it can be fun to experiment with make-up and to wear it on special occasions.

A few tools!

Here's a list of accessories you will need - a good mirror, tissues, old toothbrush (for eyebrows), several cosmetic brushes (i.e. lip, powder brush, blusher brush etc.), powder puff, pencil sharpener, cotton wool or cotton buds, cosmetic sponge.

Glossy Glossary

Concealer - used to hide spots or pimples. Available in tube, sticks or pot. Also medicated concealer available.

Foundation - gives overall colour to your face. Available in liquid, stick, creme, mousse or compact form.

Powder - gives foundation a matte finish and helps to keep make-up in place. Available in translucent and tinted, loose or compact.

Eyeshadow - available as cream, powder, or pencil. Gives colour to area around the eyes.

Blusher - used to add colour and highlight cheekbones. Available in cream, stick, loose powder or compressed powder balls.

Kohl Pencil - used to define eyes but must be kept sharpened and used with great care. Choose a soft crayon which won't pull the skin.

Mascara - used to define eyes, add thickness and also colour to eyelashes. Available in block, liquid or wand applicators.

Lipstick - adds colour, moisture and shine to lips. Use a lip pencil to make the outline then colour in with lipstick.

Lip gloss - makes lips look glossy. Can be used by itself.

The Natural Look

Often the least amount of make-up worn looks the most effective. A young face has, naturally, what make-up gives to older women. A little, though, can enhance your natural beauty!

1) Make sure you apply your make-up in a good light and have everything you need in front of you.

2) After washing and drying your face, apply the moisturiser. Hide any spots or blemishes with concealer and blend in.

3) After moisturising, apply foundation sparingly, with a sponge, dusting lightly (if necessary) with face powder.

4) Put a touch of blusher below the cheekbone. Blend gently up and out towards the hairline. Too much blusher will make you look like Coco the Clown, so take care!

5) Using a lip pencil carefully trace around the lips. Fill in with a natural-looking lipstick. Blot on a tissue then gloss over lightly.

For that Special Occasion!

For a sensational party look, your make-up will take a little longer. Allow plenty of time to get ready!

1) Tie hair back. Wash and towel face dry. Apply moisturiser and rub well in.
2) Cover any blemishes with concealer and blend in.
3) Dot foundation over your face. You can cover the lips too but not eyelids as they will turn oily. Using a damp sponge gently work the foundation evenly over the face.
4) Lightly pat translucent powder over the face. Remove excess with brush.
5) Apply some blusher over cheekbones, brushing out towards the hairline.
6) Choose a shade of eye shadow which complements your own eye colour and the clothes you are wearing. Apply the lighter shade over eyelids and blend in using a cotton bud or eye shadow brush.

Apply the darker shade to the outer half of the eye lid, and using another brush blend it in.

7) With a steady hand draw a fine pencil line close to your eyelashes and smudge it carefully using a damp cotton bud.

8) Apply mascara to top lashes. Apply a little to lower lashes (perhaps just near the corner of the eye). Leave to dry then apply a second coat.
9) Outline the shape of your lips with a lip pencil. Apply lipstick. Blot on a tissue. Repeat then apply gloss.

Don't forget, whenever you wear make-up, to remove it and cleanse your face afterwards.

BE CRAFTY

Tips

* Chemists, big department stores and places like The Body Shop always have someone you can ask about make-up. Find out from them what make-up would suit your natural colourings. What looks fantastic on your best friend could look wrong on you.

* To make eyelashes appear thicker, dust over with face powder then brush away surplus before applying mascara.

* Never share makeup, as this is a sure way of spreading infection.

* For a dramatic effect, take the shadow below your eyes and fill in above right to the eyebrow shading to a darker colour in outer corners. You could even colour the eyebrows to match.

* When applying mascara brush gently from the roots of the lashes toward the tips.

* Eyebrows can be plucked gently with a pair of slant-tipped tweezers. After brushing into shape with an old toothbrush dab a tiny bit of hair gel to hold them in place. Never pluck out hairs above the brow - only those below and over the bridge of the nose, if untidy and noticeable.

* Add some glitter dust with ordinary lip gloss in the palm of your hand then apply in the usual way.

* If you only want a hint of colour to your lashes brush it on to the tips of lashes only.

* Creamy eye shadow tends to bleed into the crease lines. To make it stay firm dust some translucent powder over before applying it.

HAIR

Hair Types

Greasy hair - is simply due to the glands producing too much sebum (oil), so wash regularly with a mild shampoo to help reduce the grease.

Dry hair - often looks dull and can be awkward to do anything with. So don't wash it too often and brush regularly to encourage more sebum. A great conditioning treatment is olive oil rubbed into the scalp.

Normal hair - if you've got it, you're lucky. Just wash and condition it regularly.

Hair-raising Problems

Dandruff - is a nuisance and looks unsightly especially if it falls on your clothes. It is a build up of dead skin cells on the scalp. There are various anti-dandruff shampoos on the market, but take care when choosing one because some are very strong. Generally the best treatment, unless you have a serious problem, is to use a mild shampoo.

Split Ends -There is nothing that can be done for these other than having the hair trimmed, but you can stop split ends occurring. Don't use too many electrical appliances on your hair, and when brushing, don't be rough, simply work any tangles free gently.

Lice - these tiny insects aren't particular whose scalp they lay eggs on. Not only are they awkward to get rid of but they're highly infectious too. The only sure way to get rid of head lice is to use one of the many lotions available from the chemist.

Washing Your Hair

1) Comb your hair to get rid of all the tangles, gels, mousse and hairspray. Wet your hair.

2) Pour a small amount of shampoo into the palm of your hand. Don't use too much otherwise it will take you ages to get all the soap rinsed off.

3) Massage the shampoo well into your scalp then rinse with plenty of warm running water until the water runs clear.

3) Rinse off with lukewarm water.

4) Pat hair dry with a towel.

Drying Your Hair

Leaving hair to dry naturally is far kinder than holding a hair drier over it. But if you do use a drier, hold it about 15cm (6") from your head and dry the hair in sections. Keep moving as you go to avoid damaging your hair.

Conditioning Your Hair

It's up to you whether or not you use a conditioner. But the time to apply it is after you've washed your hair.

1) Sparingly apply to the ends of your hair and then comb through gently.

2) Leave a minute or so.

Finger drying is easy and gives hair lots of height. Once you've combed your hair into the style you want, run your fingers through the hair quickly and at the same time hold the hair drier lifting and curling the hair into the direction you want it to keep.

Suit Yourself!

Everyone gets bored with their hairstyle and wants a complete change. But choosing a different style isn't always easy.

You've got a few things to consider:
* Is your hair texture thick, fine or medium?

* Is your face long, oval, thin or fat?

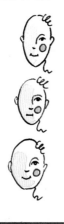

* Would you suit the hairstyle that you fancy?

* Do you like to jump out of bed in the morning and simply slap on a bit of gel, or do you have time to sit and use heated tongs?

Do-it-yourself Hairstyling

Gels - hardens and lifts at roots. Perfect for keeping slicked backed styles. Far more effective on shorter styles.

Wax - works on all types, especially curly hair, but not so good on fine. Makes hair glossier and prevents curly hair frizzing up.

Mousse - great for controlling all lengths and types of hair.

Styling Cream - adds shine to all hair types.

Hairspray - various kinds to suit hair types and will hold style firmly in place.

Colourants/Dyes - if you want to change your colour temporarily there are many wash out colourants on the market. But if you want to permanently change your hair colour, save up and get it done professionally.

covered elastic band. For the back you might well need the help of a friend!

Pop yourself under a hair drier for about an hour and then leave your hair to cool for ten minutes or so before undoing the plaits. Using a wide-toothed comb, brush through your hair - it should stay like that until at least the next wash!

Style Suggestions

Crimping - looks fantastic on long hair. It even looks good on straight shoulder length hair. If you don't own a crimping iron, plait it instead.

Divide your hair into sections, about 5cm (2") apart. Carefully plait each section and secure the end with a

A french plait can also look very effective.

Short and Sweet
You can have just as much fun with different styles for short hair!

* Sweep one side back and secure with combs or slides.

* If your hair is short and spiky on the top, and this can apply to the boys, then gel out the spikes and spray some colour on the ends for a really dramatic look.

* Shoulder length hair looks good if clipped back at the sides, or even one side and colourful bits of ribbon are attached. Or make tiny plaits all over and tie them off with covered elastic bands.

* If your hair is shaved at the back but there's more on the top, use heated bendy clips and put them all over the top. When they've set comb through and apply lots of firm hold hair spray.

* You could even crimp this length hair and then sweep it all up into a high ponytail and decorate it with ribbons.

Tips

* Don't tie hair back too tightly or hold in place with elastic bands. It will only split.

* Don't keep the drier in one position for too long or it will damage the roots of the hair.

* Don't comb tangled hair from the roots. Start a little way up easing the tangle as you go.

* Don't use other people's combs and make sure you wash yours at least once a week.

* An olive oil treatment overnight then washed out with shampoo the following morning gives hair a good conditioning treatment.

Accessories

Hair accessories are expensive but they needn't be, especially if you make your own!

* Fasten different coloured lengths of ribbon onto slides and put them into your hair.

* Cover ordinary hair grips with paint or glitter; jazz up a side comb with beads and glitter stuck onto pieces of foam; make your own huge flowers out of crepe paper and stick on to a hair grip.

* Design various shapes out of some thin foam then glue them onto hair grips.

* Weave a length of ribbon in with your plait.

* Make a broad piece of material into a bandeau and tie this around the head.

* Use a long scarf and tie it into a huge floppy bow, then if you have a fringe, pull some wisps forward and put hairspray over.

Tools for your tresses
Make sure you have a good brush (the kind with rounded quills are best), a wide toothed comb and a hair drier which has two speeds and a removable nozzle (so that more air will be distributed over the head).

* Wear a hat or beret to conceal dirty hair and decorate the hat with badges.

HANDY HINTS

Hands

Like our faces, our hands are constantly on display but sadly they are often neglected. So, to keep your hands looking good and feeling soft, follow these easy steps:

* Wear gloves in cold, icy weather.
* Massage hand cream in after you dry your hands and when washing the dishes.
* Make a habit of wearing rubber gloves when you are on washing up duty!

Nails

Nails are made from the protein keratin. Each nail is made up of six parts:

Matrix - at the very base of the nail where the cells are formed.

Nail bed - this is the skin which lies beneath the nail plate and adheres it to the finger.

Half moon - (lunula) can be seen as it hardens into the fingernail.

Nail plate - commonly known as fingernail.

Free edge - the point where it comes free before the top of the finger.

Cuticle - holds the nail in place at the base of the nail. It needs to be regularly pushed back otherwise it will come too far up the nail.

Protect Your Nails

* Keep fingernails short.
* Never use a metal nail file, they are too harsh. Instead, use the smoother edge of an emery board.
* If you suffer from weak or splitting nails, paint them with liquid nail strengthener.

2) Soak fingers in a bowl of warm soapy water for several minutes. This will help to soften the cuticles and so make pushing them back easier.

3) Massage some cuticle remover on to the fingers and, using a cotton bud, gently push the cuticles back.

Manicure

A regular manicure is good for nails. It keeps them trimmed and prevents them from splitting. All you really need is a bowl, cotton buds, an emery board and nail clippers.

1) Using an emery board, file the nail in one direction from the edge into the centre. Gently smooth off to an oval shape.

4) Snip away any loose skin around the edges of nails with some nail clippers.

5) If you don't want to wear nail polish, buff them with a nail buffer. This will give them a shine.

Pretty Polish

1) Apply a base coat. This stops polish from chipping and is ideal if used under dark colours which can often stain the nail. Start at the base of the nail and paint up the centre and then either side.

2) Choose your nail colour and starting at the little finger apply nail polish as you applied the base coat.

3) When all the nails are painted, leave them to dry before applying the second coat otherwise the polish will chip.

4) For added protection, finish off with a clear coat of nail polish.

Nails they'll Notice!

Nails needn't be painted just one colour! There are lots of things you can do to jazz them up:

* Paint half the nail one colour, when dry paint the other half another colour.

* If the nail polish is clear then brighten it up with a few dots of a darker shade.

* Sticky transfers look great on plain coloured nails.

* Be adventurous and paint only the centre part of each nail.

* Before the polish has dried sprinkle some glitter over them.

* Finally, you could try painting each finger nail a different colour!

EARS

Ear piercing is popular with both boys and girls and the current trend is to have several holes in each lobe. However, once the holes are created, ears never look quite as natural, so think carefully before having your ears pierced. **It should always be done by a professional ear piercer.** Never be tempted to let a friend do it.

Remember, if you do have pierced ears, make sure you wear clinically safe earrings and follow the after-care procedure to reduce the chance of infection which may occur. For those people who have an allergic reaction to gold, silver and alloys, there are some specially formulated hypo-allergenic earrings on the market.

Home-made Earrings
Making your own earrings can be great fun! You can create an individual look and it's much cheaper than buying them in the shops. Wear a small pair of sleepers or studs for school and keep your fashion ones for weekends!

Tips
If you already own a pair of loop earrings;

* Slip a Polo Mint through the middle of each one,

* Thread some beads through, or cut a plastic straw and slip the bendy part to sit along the middle of the earring.

* A plastic-coated paper-clip will look eye-catching but several can look really dramatic.

* Draw and cut out a small shape like a fish or a piece of fruit, on to a piece of sponge and pierce this on to the loop.

If you really want a pair of long, dangling earrings, thread tiny beads onto several lengths of cotton, knot them together at the top and tie them all around the centre of each loop.

Creative with Clip-On's

There is no reason why you can't have fun designing and wearing clip-on earrings. Craft shops generally sell clip-on and screw-on earring backs at quite reasonable prices.

* Trace a shape, say a strawberry, onto a piece of sponge. Cut it out and stick this in place on an earring back with good all-purpose glue.

* Trace and colour the shape of the sun or stars on a piece of card. Cut out, paste one side and sprinkle with glitter. When quite dry, glue the plain side onto an earring base.

* Using a circle of cardboard as a base, mould pieces of coloured clay into a decorative design. Glue these onto the card and the card to the earring base.

Using the screw-on earrings you could, more or less, adopt the similar designs for pierced earrings.

These are just a few ideas but you're bound to have plenty of fun thinking up your own! Look out for interesting buttons and beads in glass, wood and plastic to thread onto earring bases in bright clusters or exotic dangling tiers.

FEET

The Bad News
Did you know that 7 out of 10 people have some kind of foot problem before they reach their twenties? Some of the problems stem from childhood. A pair of ill-fitting shoes can result in lasting problems and huge discomfort when you're a little older.

Keep Feet Fit!
Yes, feet need exercise. Give your overworked feet a chance to breathe and, when indoors, walk around barefoot.

The Good News
Trainers are popular with both girls and boys, which is just as well as they're ideal for your feet, giving them space to breathe and grow.

IN SHAPE

Looking good and feeling good gives you confidence in yourself. It makes you feel able to do things that you may otherwise shy away from. Not everyone can afford to keep up with the latest fashion trends. Not everyone wants to! What your friend looks good in may look odd on you. It's all to do with body shape.

There are basically three body shapes. Some people may fit into one category, but most of us are a combination:

Ectomorph - slim build, may eat a lot of food but burns it up, so never seems to put weight on.

Mesomorph - medium build, naturally slim with a lot of muscle and bone, not much fat.

Endomorph - heavy build, well covered, but not fat.

Tips

* Whatever your body shape, you can change the way you look by using a few simple 'tricks'!

* Vertical stripes on a sweater or dress gives a taller and much slimmer appearance whereas horizontal stripes have the opposite effect.

* If you look stringy and could do with filling out around the waist, full skirts will give your body shape the look you want. For someone who is on the large size, plain fabrics will complement their shape, whereas an attractive printed design does wonders for the smaller figure.

* The same applies to printed fabrics. A larger person should keep away from a bright coloured fabric with big designs and wear a darker coloured fabric with a small pattern over.

Just Your Colour

Colour is the best way to express your individuality. But not all colours suit everyone. Knowing your colour is all a case of trial and error. Get together with several friends and match up each other's garments until you find the colours which suit your skin and hair colourings best.

Start a Style

Once you know which colours suit you and what clothes make the best of your shape, you can experiment with styles to find a look that will say something about yourself!

Sort Out

If you spend most of the week wearing school uniform, the clothes in your wardrobe will be mainly for weekends and your leisure time. Before you splash all your pocket money or savings on some new clothes, take a good look at what you already have in your wardrobe. Are there items which have not seen the light of day for months? Perhaps there's something looking slightly tatty or worse for wear? If that's the case, you've three options: throw it out, give it away, or re-design it.

Providing the material of the garment is in reasonable condition and will withstand 'revamping', then don't waste time - get out the needle and thread!

Home-Made Fashion

Adapting your current wardrobe can be fun and makes sense when funds are low.

* If you've a cardigan with boring buttons remove them and invest in some bright ones.

* Or give a jumper a face lift by sewing small bows and buttons all over, make a fringe out of lengths of wool and sew them along the front and back.

* An old shirt can be recycled if it is torn into strips measuring 2.5cm (1") thick. Tie them together and then roll up into a ball. The next step is to persuade mum to knit it into a simple T-shaped top for you.

* Instead of wearing a plain jacket why not wear a thick shirt as a jacket instead.

* Two shirts, one worn on top of the other, look very eye catching especially if one is plain and the other patterned.

* An old jumper worn away at the elbows can be given a new lease of life either by sewing elbow pads on or alternatively cutting them off and edging with braid to make it a short sleeved jumper.

* Tie and dye an old plain tee shirt, cut it to a cropped version, make tears in and then wear it on top of a different coloured tee shirt. You could always remove the sleeves and leave them ragged or sew in another pair from another tee shirt.

* Over-sized sweaters and cardigans are fashionable - and warmer too.

* Beads or sequins sewn on to a sweater or plain dress can give it a new trendy look.

* Old pyjamas make fun summer trousers with the sleeves and legs rolled up.

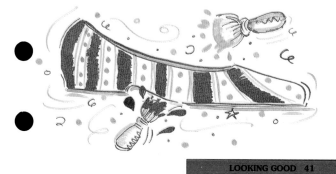

* Mens' clothes can be turned into something different. Large shirts and sweaters can be worn as mini dresses if belted and worn with a thick pair of wooden tights or leggings underneath.

* Inject life into an old pair of shoes or sandshoes, decorate with sequins and glitter, or dye them but make sure you do a test piece first.

Shopping Around

Extending your wardrobe with the minimum of cost is easier than you think:

* The Sales can be a good way to get a bargain for your wardrobe, but they're also the worst thing to tempt 'impulse buys' - things you buy on the spur of the moment, only to find they don't go with any of your clothes once you get home!

* Army and Navy Surplus stores might seem an unlikely place to shop, but they stock quite a wide range of inexpensive sweatshirts, hats, jumpers, etc. which, with a badge or scarf, can be given a bright facelift.

* Local charity shops and jumble sales sell a range of second hand items, including clothes. Some are very clean but it's always wise to wash an item of clothing or accessory well before wearing it. You may find the ideal thing at a price you can afford.

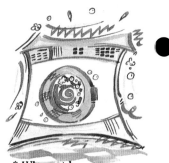

* Why not have a clothes swapping day with some school friends? Everyone has something in their wardrobe they will want to exchange. But do check this out with parents beforehand.

* You may be surprised to find some fashionable 'togs' amongst other wardrobes in your house. But do ask permission before 'borrowing' anything!

Accessories

These are an important part of any fashionable wardrobe. Hang on to bits and pieces long enough and chances are they will return as a fashion accessory within a few seasons.

Belts - can make the most boring outfit look up-to-the-minute. A belt worn loosely over hips can give a totally new look to a long sweater or a plain dress. So can a belt buckled tightly and worn around the waistband of a plain skirt.

Improvise! Use a scarf or a tie as a belt - it can look just right.

Belt Building

Plait several lengths of coloured string together and tie securely at either end.

Cotton reels painted and threaded on to a length of cord (long enough to lie loosely around your waist) are fun. For a disco look, sprinkle them with glitter.

If mum has an old piece of silk twist curtain cord she no longer uses, this will make a colourful belt.

For a great unusual belt effect, cut out two lengths of clear plastic approximately 5cm (2") thick, almost long enough to fit around your waist. Save up all your old postage stamps and when you have sufficient to fit along the length of plastic glue them in place.

Stick the other piece of plastic over the top and, when dry, cover each end with a strip of coloured sticky tape. To fasten the belt, punch two holes at either end of the belt and thread some string through. You'll have a belt that will be the envy of all your friends and it will certainly be a good topic of conversation, especially if you have some foreign stamps.

For good fashion fun, be inventive!

Gloves - Not just to keep your hands cosy in winter - they make a special outfit look 'finished off'. Check if gran has an old pair of lace ones, or you may be able to pick a pair up cheaply in a jumble sale. Either wear them the same colour or dye them to go with your outfit.

* Cut the fingers off an old pair of gloves and sew the ends over to stop them fraying, add some colourful beads or sequins on to the back.

* Transform a plain pair of gloves into a glitzy pair, thread several different coloured pieces of ribbon around.

* Or, with plain gloves, be creative and fabric paint each finger a different colour or paint one side black and the other white. If you want to be really daring, cut small shapes out all over.

* If you are going to a disco, every trendsetter needs a pair of gloves! If you can find an old pair of long evening gloves, liven them up with chunky bracelets or wear glitzy fashion rings on several fingers.

Scarves - come in so many different colours, sizes and materials that it would be crazy not to try and include them in your new styles!

* Wrap a long glittery scarf several times around your wrist.

* Dress your head in a turban scarf and secure a classy brooch in the middle.

* Throw a large square scarf over one shoulder and up around the other, then pin a brooch in.

* Change the look of a skirt and loosely drape a square scarf around your hips.

* A scarf knotted loosely around your neck with the ends hanging looks stylish worn over a jumper.

* Try this! Take two large square scarves, tack them together leaving space for your head and arms, and there you have a slip over top.

* Silky Indian scarves are popular worn around the head as a bandeau, and can look stunning if tied at the collar of a plain blouse.

Jazz it up with Jewellry!

A pair of long strings of coloured beads can be worn in a number of exciting ways, as a single strand knotted near the bottom, worn back to front so it looks like a choker, several in different coloured lengths, or braided together.

* To make your own chunky bracelets cut a washing-up liquid bottle into 2.5cm (1") pieces. Paint each one and before they have dried cover with glitter or edge with coloured sticky tape.

* Turn one of them into a snake by cutting a shaped head at one end - they look great halfway up the arm.
* Liven up the lapel of a plain jacket with a clip-on earring, you could do the same on the collar of a plain blouse.

* Transform an imitation brass door plate into a brooch or even a pendant.
* Old watches, or Albert chains, add their own mark to an outfit.
* Studs attached to the collar of a plain blouse can give it a new stunning look and don't forget, braces are also very stylish worn on trousers and skirts.

Hats - are both trendy and stylish, so if there is an old trilby stuffed in the attic, get it out!

* Glue a length of coloured ribbon around the middle and stick a small feather in the side.

* Straw hats can be brightened up and even dyed a different colour or re-vamped with artificial flowers and a huge flowing ribbon on the side.

* Liven up a plain coloured beret with a classy brooch.

* If the hat has seen better times then cut out the top so that your hair can flow out.

So, it's up to you. Discover your own style, and the clothes which look best on you. Remember which colours suit you, too - and enjoy experimenting at home. Fashion is not a set of rules - you decide what goes, and you don't have to spend money to change your clothes around. Have fun *Looking Good!*